The Inside Story
Igloo

Dana Meachen Rau

Marshall Cavendish
Benchmark
New York

Inside an Igloo

1 airhole

2 bed

3 snow block

4 tunnel

5 window

The *Inuit* built snow homes on the *tundra*.

They called their homes igloos.

First, they cut blocks of snow.

They used a tool made from whale bone.

They laid the blocks in a circle.

Then they cut some of the blocks on a *slant*.

They added blocks around the circle.

The circle was smaller each time around.

The walls grew higher.

At the top, the walls grew closer.

They put the last block in the top.

Then they dug out a doorway.

They built a *tunnel* to the
door.

They filled the cracks with
snow.

They cut a hole in the top of the igloo.

This would let in some air.

They cut a window in front.

They filled it with ice.

Inside, they built a bed of snow.

They covered it with soft fur.

They lit an oil lamp.

It kept the igloo warm.

The walls became ice.

The igloo was a strong, warm home.

Inside an Igloo

blocks

circle

doorway

tunnel

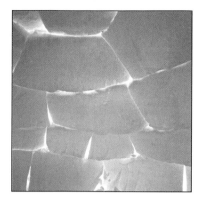
walls

window

Challenge Words

Inuit (I-new-wuht) People who lived in or near the Arctic.

slant A side or line that is high on one end and low on the other.

tundra (TUN-druh) A large, flat area without trees in the Arctic.

tunnel (TUN-uhl) A low, narrow passageway.

Index

Page numbers in **boldface** are illustrations.

About the Author

Dana Meachen Rau is an author, editor, and illustrator. A graduate of Trinity College in Hartford, Connecticut, she has written more than one hundred fifty books for children, including nonfiction, biographies, early readers, and historical fiction. She lives with her family in Burlington, Connecticut.

Reading Consultants

Nanci Vargus, Ed.D. is an Assistant Professor of Elementary Education at the University of Indianapolis.

Beth Walker Gambro received her M.S. Ed. Reading from the University of St. Francis, Joliet, Illinois.

With thanks to Nanci Vargus, Ed.D. and
Beth Walker Gambro, reading consultants

Marshall Cavendish Benchmark
Marshall Cavendish
99 White Plains Road
Tarrytown, New York 10591-9001
www.marshallcavendish.us

Library of Congress Cataloging-in-Publication Data

Rau, Dana Meachen 1971–
Igloo / by Dana Meachen Rau.
p. cm. — (Bookworms. The inside story)
Includes index.
ISBN-13: 978-0-7614-2273-0
ISBN-10: 0-7614-2273-0
1. Igloos—Juvenile literature. 2. Eskimos—Dwellings. I. Title. II.
Series.
E99.E7R23 2006
693'.91089971—dc22
2005031262

Photo Research by Anne Burns Images

Cover Photo by Alaska Stock/Jeff Schultz

The photographs in this book are used with permission and through the courtesy of:
Corbis: pp. 1, 25 B.Glanzmann/zefa; pp. 13, 31tl Staffan Widstrand/zefa; p. 27 Stuart Westmorland.
North Wind Picture Archives: p. 5. Woodfin Camp: pp. 7, 9, 11, 15, 30tl, 30tr, 30bl William Strode.
Alaska Stock: pp. 17, 30br Jeff Schultz. Getty Images: pp. 19, 21, 31tr.
Bridgeman Art Library: p. 23 The Stapleton Collection.

Printed in Malaysia
1 3 5 6 4 2